A Day With a
Pueblo

A PUEBLO

by Tito E. Naranjo

Illustrations by Giorgio Bacchin

RP

Runestone Press/Minneapolis

A Division of the Lerner Publishing Group

This book is for my son and grandchildren: Jensedo, Tamara, Johnathan, Rachel, Sophia, and Elizabeth. They bring me joy. I thank Bernice, my wife, who is from Taos Pueblo, for teaching me indirectly what I know about the pueblo. We are both Tanoan speakers, but she is Tiwa and I am Tewa, so we speak English to one another.

All words that appear in **bold** are explained in the glossary that starts on page 43.

This edition first published in the United States in 2000 by Runestone Press.

Runestone Press, A Division of the Lerner Publishing Group
241 First Avenue North, Minneapolis, MN 55401 U.S.A.

Website: www.lernerbooks.com

Captions translated by Dominique Clift.

Photos are used courtesy of Editoriale Jaca Book, Milan (Silvia Vassena): 8, 10, 11, 12, 13 (middle), 15 (insets); (Ermano Leso): 9, 13 (top), 14 (insets); (Stefano Raffa): 14, 15; Franco Meli, Milan: 13 (bottom).

Library of Congress Cataloging-in-Publication Data

Naranjo, Tito.
[Giornata con un indiano Taos. English]
A Pueblo / by Tito E. Naranjo ; illustrations by Giorgio Bacchin.
p.   cm. — (A day with)
Includes bibliographical references.
Summary: Describes a day in the life of a Pueblo elder.
ISBN 0-8225-1919-4 (lib. bdg. : alk. paper)
1. Taos aged—Juvenile literature. 2. Taos Indians—Social life and customs—Juvenile literature. 3. Taos Pueblo (N.M.)—Social life and customs—Juvenile literature. [1. Taos Indians. 2. Indians of North America—Southwest, New. 3. Old age.]
I. Bacchin, Giorgio, ill. II. Title. III. Series: Day with—
E99.T2N37   2000
305.26—DC21   98—54143

Manufactured in the United States of America
1 2 3 4 5 6 — JR — 05 04 03 02 01 00

CONTENTS

INTRODUCTION

The ancestors of Native Americans, also called American Indians, inhabited North America before Europeans arrived in the 1500s. North America ranges from tropical (hot and lush) to arctic (cold and snowy) in climate. Bounded by oceans to the east and west, the continent is crossed by wild rivers and lined with jutting mountain ranges. Plains stretch across North America, and huge lakes dot its surface. Deserts and woodlands spread over many regions.

Early Native American cultures adapted to the environments in which they lived. In coastal regions, Native Americans hunted sea creatures and collected shellfish from the ocean waters. Inland river and lake Indians netted or speared freshwater fish in creeks, lakes, and rivers. On the wide, grassy plains, Native Americans hunted buffalo by throwing spears, by shooting arrows, or by luring the animals over cliffs. In the forests, some folks hunted deer and small mammals. In other parts of the continent, farmers grew corn, beans, and squash in small plots or large fields. Houses and clothing varied, too.

Native American belief systems also reflected environments. Some religions revolved around animals and successful hunting, the weather, the changing seasons, or the ocean. Many belief systems were **animist,** which gave every object a spirit.

Over centuries, Native Americans traveled from one end of the continent to the other and sometimes back again. These movements are remembered in the oral histories of many Indian nations and can be traced in the groups of languages that people speak. Ancient American Indians spoke more than 200 distinct languages, with thousands of dialects.

Some North American civilizations grew into huge empires ruled by powerful leaders. Large populations flooded cities that were later deserted. Small towns and villages flourished, as did nomadic communities. No one was rich or poor in some cultures, but in others some members lived in splendor while their neighbors shivered in small dwellings.

Trade routes linked people across the continent, bringing goods and new ideas from faraway places. The idea of pottery traveled from modern-day Mexico to what would later become the southwestern United States. Other people may have traded buffalo hides or meat for farm produce.

With the arrival of Europeans, life changed for all Native Americans. But the Pueblo people of modern-day New Mexico have preserved many elements of their traditional lifestyle, while successfully adapting to changing times.

Series Editors

PART ONE

THE WORLD OF THE PUEBLO

The Pueblo people live in 19 **pueblos** (towns or villages) that dot New Mexico. Taos, the northernmost pueblo, sits on a sagebrush-covered plateau that is 7,000 feet high. Northeastward rises Pueblo Peak, which the people of Taos Pueblo call Mawholo. **Shrines** make this mountain a sacred place. The foothills of the Sangre de Christo Mountains sit in the east. The San Juan Mountains are northward. High in these mountains is **Blue Lake,** which has religious significance for the Pueblo Indians. Westward, the **Rio Grande** runs through a deep gorge in the plateau.

The Native Americans who live at Taos and at the other pueblos share many aspects of their cultures, such as similar social structures. Their religious practices and architectural styles also have much in common. Traditionally, most Pueblos were farmers who grew corn, beans, and squash. But the people of Taos combined agriculture with hunting buffalo and interacted with many other Native American peoples.

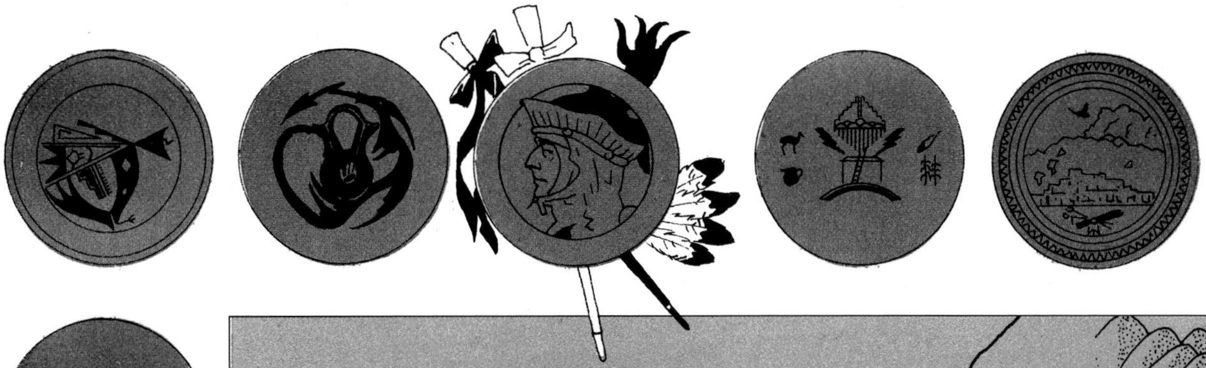

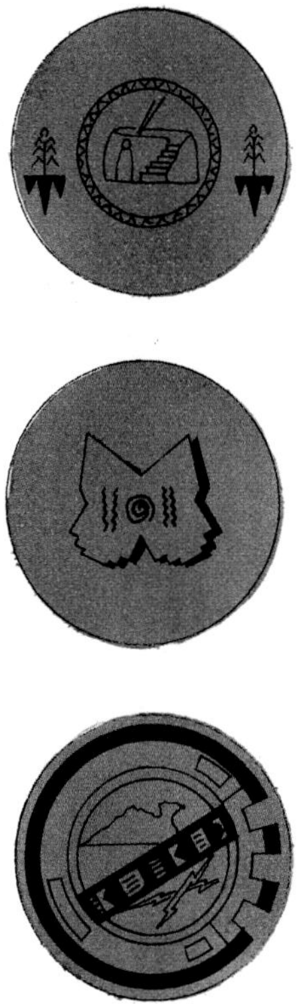

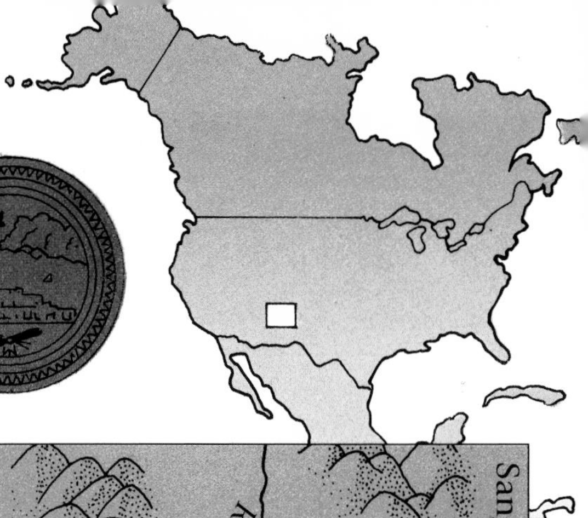

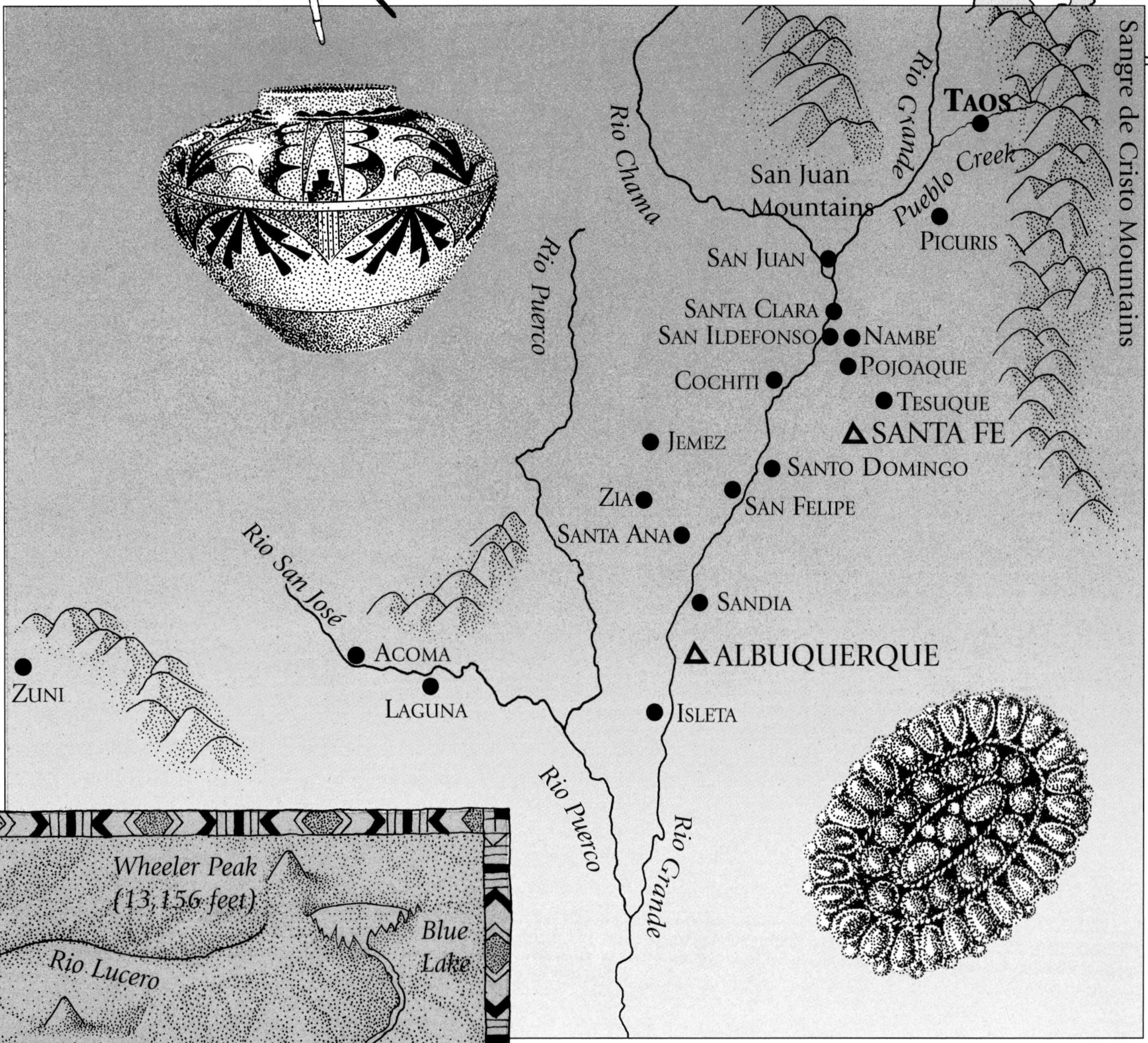
Sangre de Cristo Mountains
Rio Grande
Taos
Rio Chama
San Juan Mountains
Pueblo Creek
Picuris
San Juan
Rio Puerco
Santa Clara
San Ildefonso
Nambe'
Pojoaque
Cochiti
Tesuque
Santa Fe
Jemez
Santo Domingo
Zia
San Felipe
Santa Ana
Rio San José
Sandia
Albuquerque
Acoma
Zuni
Laguna
Isleta
Rio Puerco
Rio Grande

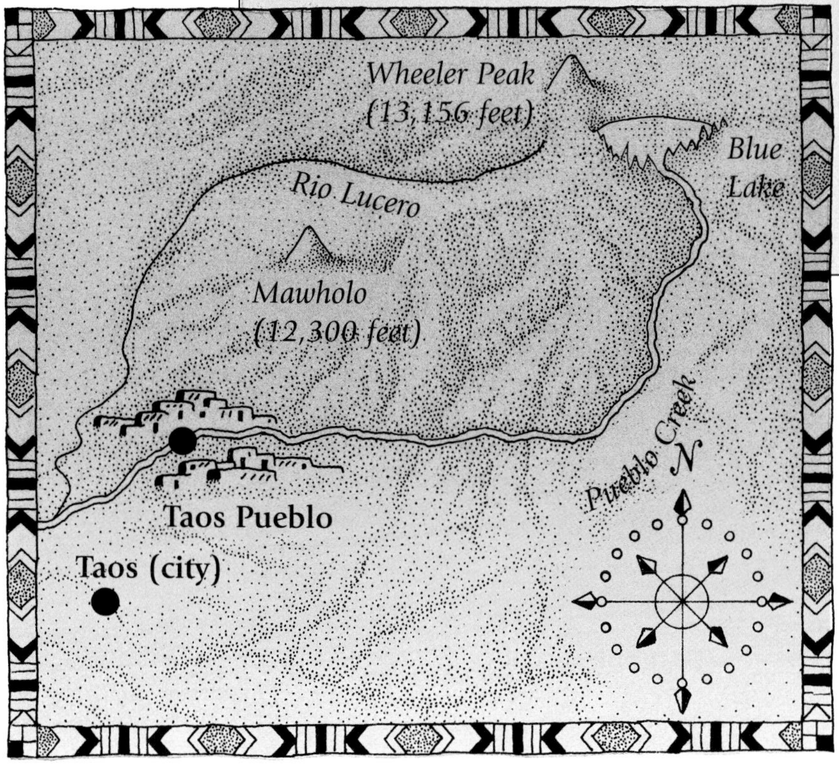
Wheeler Peak
(13,156 feet)
Blue Lake
Rio Lucero
Mawholo
(12,300 feet)
Pueblo Creek
N
Taos Pueblo
Taos (city)

Stylized symbols represent the eight northernmost pueblos, which are (counterclockwise from top right) *Taos, Picuris, San Juan, Santa Clara, San Ildefonso, Nambe', Pojoaque, and Tesuque. The map shows the 19 villages inhabited by Pueblo Indians. The vase* (top left) *was crafted at San Ildefonso, a pueblo known for its ceramics. At Zuni Pueblo, artisans make silver and jewelry* (bottom right). (Inset) *Taos Pueblo is near a modern town of the same name.*

The Sangre de Christo Mountains are visible from Taos Pueblo (top left). *Narrow passageways separate apartments at South House* (middle left). *This young woman lives at Taos Pueblo* (bottom left). *Mawholo rises behind North House* (above).

The Pueblo speak three different languages—Keresan, Zunian, and Tanoan. Tanoan is divided into the Tiwa, Tewa, and Towa dialects. The people of Taos speak Tiwa. Residents of Picuris, Sandia, and Isleta also speak Tiwa.

Archaeologists estimate that Native Americans began to build Taos Pueblo between the eleventh and thirteenth centuries. People have lived in this village ever since, making it one of the oldest continuously inhabited settlements in North America.

Two large structures of **adobe** brick dominate the pueblo, which is crossed by Pueblo Creek. The creek not only provides water but separates the settlement into two sections. Five stories high, Humo (North House) stands north of Pueblo Creek. Huokwimo

(Above) *Ladders make it easy to move between the many levels of Humo, and brightly painted doors afford privacy.*

(South House), which rises four stories high, sits to the south of the waterway. A ruin of the San Geronimo **mission** church, a cemetery, and many smaller homes are nearby. Three round, underground ceremonial chambers called **kivas** lie on each side of Pueblo Creek. An adobe wall circles Taos Pueblo.

The pueblo looks much as it did when an early European explorer named Hernando de Alvarado described it in 1541. He wrote, "The houses are built very close together and have five or six floors. Three of these have mud walls, and two or more of the upper [rooms] have thin, wooden walls. The floors are smaller at the upper levels. Every floor has a small terrace. . . . " But some things have changed at Taos Pueblo. In ancient times, people entered the buildings through holes in the roofs. These days residents like glass windows and wooden doors. Cooks prefer rounded, outdoor ovens (called *hornos*) and wood-burning stoves with chimneys to open fires. But some

Tourists come to Taos to visit the kivas and other ancient buildings.

modern conveniences, such as electricity, are forbidden within the pueblo's outer wall.

The people of Taos work hard to keep their pueblo in good shape. The adobe that covers the walls can be washed away by abundant rain, or it might crack from cold and snow. The people who live in a house repair it as the Pueblo have done for hundreds of years. Residents first apply a thick coat of adobe. Then they smooth it with a sheepskin.

No distinction exists between daily life and religious life at the pueblos. The people feel a special connection with the water, the earth, and the sky and they typically begin the day with prayers. Ceremonial and religious life are both organized around kivas. In fact, those who live at Taos Pueblo call themselves *teutho t'yono*, which means "people of the kiva."

Between the ages of six and ten, boys and girls become members of a kiva. Boys soon leave their parents to begin 18 months of kiva training, when they live in the pueblo buildings and in the kiva itself. Boys are initiated into the beliefs and ways

Blue Lake (above) *is a sacred place where rituals are performed. A graveyard* (right) *surrounds the ruins of a mission at Taos Pueblo. A new church* (bottom) *was built in the 1800s.*

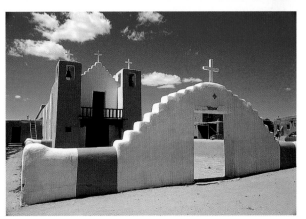

of the pueblo during this time. The training helps preserve the Tiwa language, beliefs, and cultural values such as community work. Men undergo this training again at various points in their lives, to reinforce the beliefs learned as youngsters.

At Taos, the population is split into **moieties** (two groups of equal size). Members of the north kivas make up one moiety, and members of the south kivas make up the other. The Pueblo people choose leaders from the moieties, which also compete in footraces, in dances, and in ritual activities. Many pueblos, including Taos, have a **cacique,** a religious leader who leads the most important kiva. Helping the cacique is a **war chief** who enforces the rules of the pueblo. Several war captains are selected from each moiety. The war captains are in charge of making sure that events—ceremonial and social dances, hunts, and footraces—are conducted correctly.

Drums and drumming play an important role in ceremonial life at Taos. Drum making is a lengthy process that requires a great deal of skill. A craftsperson can spend 30 hours making a single drum!

Finding a fallen poplar tree is the first step. Next, people from the pueblo use a chainsaw to slice it into sections. With great effort, workers roll the wood to a workshop, where a craftsperson hollows the trunk by hand. Artisans cut it to size and polish the wood to make a drum frame. The drum-maker attaches the skin of a deer or an ox across the hole —one piece of leather across the top and one across the bottom. Using pincers, the worker stretches the

Drums provide music for ceremonial events. It takes great skill for an artisan to make a drum from a fallen tree.

leather taut and fixes it to the drum frame with nails. Leather thongs are threaded through the nail holes in both skins. When the artisan tightens the thongs, the tension of the leather changes. This adjusts the sound that the drum makes when played.

Foods, such as chili pepper stew and bread baked in a horno, are important parts of Pueblo Indian festivities. Generosity and communal meals are valued. Many of the celebrations are public and attract tourists. Corn, a traditional staple food, figures prominently in the Pueblo Indian tradition. Many villages hold a solemn corn dance. At Taos Pueblo, San Antonio Day (a festival borrowed from Christian, Spanish-speaking settlers) is celebrated with the corn dance. Dancers hope for a bountiful harvest of corn and for good times.

Corn, a grain native to the Americas, is a traditional staple of the Pueblo Indian diet. Hornos, or domed ovens, and doors are commonly seen at the pueblos. In former times, the people used open fires and entered their homes through the roof.

Although the characters in this story are fictional, the Pueblo Indian way of life is very real. For hundreds of years, the Pueblo people farmed the arid land of the **Southwest** and hunted deer, elk, and rabbit for meat. But in the 1500s, explorers from Spain's colony of Mexico arrived. The newcomers claimed the region for Spain and named it New Mexico. Spanish army officials made the Native Americans lay roads, put up buildings, produce goods, work as domestic slaves, and toil in mines and on farms. Christian **missionaries** forced the Pueblo people to build and to attend mission churches. They outlawed the traditional Pueblo religion. Most Native Americans began to follow Christianity, but many secretly continued their own faith. A blend of Christian and Pueblo ceremonies and beliefs developed. Mexican farmers, traders, and ranchers arrived and established friendly relationships with the Pueblo people. Most missionaries eventually left the area, so the Pueblo again practiced their own religion in public.

In the 1800s, Mexico and New Mexico won their independence from Spain. Mexico and the United States were soon at war. When the United States won, it acquired New Mexico. In January 1847, Mexican settlers and Native Americans began the Taos Revolt against the new government by murdering New Mexico's governor. The U.S. military defeated the Taos residents, and New Mexico became part of the United States in 1848. Settlers from the eastern United States soon claimed much Pueblo Indian territory. In 1906 the United States made Blue Lake and the surrounding area part of Carson National Forest.

Throughout the twentieth century, the Pueblo coped with constantly changing U.S. government policies. In 1910 and 1922, U.S. laws restored Native American land and paid for some land not returned. In 1948 the Pueblo were granted the right to vote. The government's return of nearly 50,000 acres of Carson National Forest, including Blue Lake, in 1971 was a Pueblo triumph.

The Pueblo people maintain their culture in changing times. Some Native Americans live at pueblos and preserve elements of their age-old lifestyle. Let's spend a day with Aspen Deer, a modern elder at Taos Pueblo, as he prepares for a holiday and reminisces about times past.

PART TWO

A DAY WITH ASPEN DEER, A PUEBLO ELDER

**A**spen Deer woke while the morning light was faint. Although it was June, the air felt chilly. Careful not to awaken his wife, Blue Sun, he dressed quickly and walked outdoors. He slowly climbed the ladder that lay against the side of his house. When he stood on the flat roof, he faced the mountains to the east, where Pueblo Creek flowed from Blue Lake. Above Taos Pueblo, he saw the massive peak of Mawholo. With his arms outstretched, Aspen Deer began to chant a prayer.

Aspen Deer is my name
Sun Father above and Earth Mother below
Spirits of the North, West, South, and East
Thank you this day
For the strength of my legs
For the strength of my arms
For breath you have given me this day
For the strength of good thoughts
For the well-being of my family
For the well-being of my people
Give us love and respect for each other today
May I be in harmony with those around me
Give me strength this day.

Aspen Deer gently moved his arms toward his chest, symbolically pulling the breath of the sky, the earth, and the sun into him. Aspen Deer had said this prayer every morning since he had reached manhood more than 50 years ago. It would guide him throughout the day.

From the rooftop, Aspen Deer surveyed Taos Pueblo. He admired the clear waters of Pueblo Creek, which flowed like an artery of life between Humo and Huokwimo, and he noticed pickup trucks parked near the banks. The creek began in the mountains where the sacred Blue Lake lay. He imagined how the village would look from high above—the geometric shapes of the buildings, the crumbling church ruin, and the bright pickup trucks near the creek ranged across the dry brown earth.

Blue Sun and Aspen Deer didn't live on the pueblo all year round. Most of the time, they shared a small house not too far away. They were visiting the pueblo to prepare for the next day's festival, San Antonio Day, when the dancers would perform the Corn Dance.

Aspen Deer saw a group of men on horseback leaving the pueblo, and he guessed that they were going on a community rabbit hunt. He spotted his daughter's son, Jerome, among them. Because of San Antonio Day tomorrow, hunters would give men named Antonio and women named Antonia the rabbits killed during the hunt.

Blue Sun and Aspen Deer had arrived at their small house at Taos Pueblo yesterday evening. Blue Sun would spend the day cleaning the house. Aspen Deer planned to help dig soil away from the walls of the old mission church. He also planned to help clear a room on the fifth level of Humo, so that it would be ready for repairs.

The morning was still cool. Wisps of smoke began to curl from his chimney and from a few others. Aspen Deer climbed down the ladder. Inside Blue Sun stirred a pan of cornmeal gruel that cooked on the wood-burning stove.

Aspen Deer took a bucket in each hand and walked south to Pueblo Creek, where he filled the pails with clear water. When he returned, they ate a simple breakfast of coffee, gruel, and fried meat. After they had finished eating, Blue Sun filled a canvas canteen with water while Aspen Deer found his shovel. Then he walked to the former church, which had been a ruin for more than a hundred years, although the people of Taos still used the cemetery.

Yellow Elk, a man in his late fifties, was already hard at work. Aspen Deer watched him shovel dirt from the walls that surrounded the old church. Earlier Yellow Elk had wrapped the blanket all Pueblo men wear around his head to keep off the sun. He took it off when he got too hot.

Although the walls were only waist-high, the rubble around them was deep. Because they had both completed kiva training, Aspen Deer greeted his friend with a phrase that meant they shared a close bond.

Soon after, Aspen Deer began to work alongside Yellow Elk. A group of tourists approached. The visitors asked the two men about the old church. As Yellow Elk continued to work, Aspen Deer leaned on his shovel and spoke.

"Long time ago, during the Taos Revolt, my grandfather shot at your grandfather here. Your grandfathers won because they shot a strong gun—a cannon. My grandfather hid in the back of this church; he was killed right here."

The tourists thanked Aspen Deer and strolled off to view other parts of Taos Pueblo. But Aspen Deer's thoughts turned to the revolt's history. In January 1847, settlers from Mexico and Indians had murdered the U.S. governor of New Mexico. When three U.S. Army regiments arrived, Native Americans hid in the church, which the U.S. forces bombarded with cannon shells until it collapsed. About 500 people had died.

Aspen Deer returned to his labors. By the time the hot sun was nearly overhead, Aspen Deer and Yellow Elk had dug a trench that followed the wall behind the old church. Aspen Deer guessed that they were near the ruins of the old rectory (the priests' house). Aspen Deer's shovel clanged against a metal object. He pulled out a dirt-encrusted steel ball. Aspen Deer decided to bring the object home to show Blue Sun.

Just before noon, Yellow Elk and Aspen Deer decided to stop digging for the day. Both men were hungry, and the sun was hot. They agreed to meet at Humo after lunch. Aspen Deer walked home, carrying the ball, as well as a blackened spoon and a chain of beads that he had unearthed.

**B**ack in the cool, dark house, he showed Blue Sun the steel ball. She read the words: "Pittsburgh, Pennsylvania, June 1840."

"This must be one of the cannonballs that the Americans used to shell the church," Aspen Deer said in Tiwa. Blue Sun examined the glass beads before she picked up the black spoon. Blue Sun said that tarnish caused the dark color and that it was a silver spoon. She noticed the word "London" engraved on the underside of the handle. Aspen Deer placed his findings on a shelf, next to the clock radio that ran on batteries.

The two had just sat down to eat lunch when their grandson Jerome entered the house. The boy joined his grandparents at the table and ate hungrily, telling them about his rabbit-hunting expedition.

Aspen Deer spoke of the rabbit hunts that he had gone on in his youth. In those days, Aspen Deer told Jerome, the Pueblo men had hunted on foot, not from horseback. They had walked in large circles on the sagebrush plateaus that stretched to the west of Taos Pueblo. The circle of men tightened until the hunters walked next to one another. Rabbits found themselves caught in the middle of a circle, where the animals were easy to spear with sharp **throwing sticks.** He told Jerome that hunters used the same method on the community deer hunts the Pueblo held up in the mountains each February and March.

Jerome's interest in the traditional culture of the Pueblo pleased Aspen Deer. With so many people living far away from Taos, youngsters didn't always learn the old ways. Many kids didn't even know how to speak Tiwa. Aspen Deer's grandchildren knew both English and Tiwa, so Aspen Deer spoke to them in Tiwa.

After lunch Aspen Deer grabbed his shovel and his blanket and walked toward Humo. Yellow Elk was waiting at the foot of a ladder, which they climbed to the structure's second level, the home of two or three families. They next passed the third level, where boys who were undergoing kiva training often ate and slept.

He was glad to see people busy preparing for San Antonio Day. Aspen Deer wondered how much longer the age-old traditions would last. Life at the pueblo had changed a lot since his own childhood, when most of the teutho t'yono lived at Taos Pueblo. Sometimes the changes worried him. He didn't know who would repair Humo and Huokwimo in the future.

The two men reached a small room at the back of Humo. Yellow Elk opened the wooden door, which swung on **rawhide** hinges. Both men had to duck when they passed through the doorway into the dark, dusty room. Some sunshine entered through a window high in the wall near the door. The two men propped the door open to allow in more light.

No one had lived in this room for over a hundred years. Aspen Deer inhaled the musty odor of earthen walls, which reminded him of the smell inside the kivas. Log beams called *vigas* supported the cracked and damaged roof. From the vigas hung a pole, with a blanket hanging over it. The room was painted in the traditional way, with **thun** on the upper parts of walls and brown plaster on the lower parts.

Next to the door Aspen Deer noticed a "dust boy," a bowl built flush into the dirt floor. When people had lived in this room, women swept loose dirt into the dust boy. Since then the use of wood and other floor coverings had made dust boys rare.

It was easy to spot why the room needed some repairs. The wall had partly collapsed in the corner, creating a pile of dirt and rubble. Aspen Deer began to shovel it away, but his shovel hit something hard. He dug carefully with his hands until he had uncovered pieces of fire-blackened pottery. Aspen Deer fitted the parts together and removed a pocket cloth from his waist. He wrapped the potsherds (fragments) snugly in the cloth. The jar would be easy to repair.

Yellow Elk found a braided, nine-foot-long strip of rawhide hanging from a viga. Yellow Elk said, "This rope was made of hide, a long time ago when the buffalo roamed the plains."

Aspen Deer knew that this meant that the rope was old—buffalo hadn't wandered free for a century or so. The two men finished clearing the room while the sun was still high. In a few days, other men would replace the roof and repair the wall. As Aspen Deer and Yellow Elk climbed down the ladders to the ground, they saw a Pueblo leader standing above them at the top of Humo. In a sing-song voice, he cried out the names of those who were to dance tomorrow. People paused in their work to listen to the list of names.

The tightly bound potsherds in his hands made Aspen Deer think of Red Stone, his oldest daughter, and Blue Flower, his mother. The older woman had given Red Stone her name, which referred to the smooth river stones used to burnish un-fired pottery. As a child, Red Stone had spent summers with Blue Flower, who made pottery for storage, for carrying water, for cooking, and to trade.

The older woman had taught her granddaughter how to gather the clay for which Taos pottery was famous. The clay contained flakes of **silica,** a mineral that sparkled like gold on the fired pots. Potters from southern pueblos came to Taos for that clay.

Blue Flower had taught young Red Stone how to add temper—volcanic ash, sand, or parts of broken pots—to make clay stronger, more flexible, and easier to mold. Red Stone had learned how to form jars, bowls, and other objects and how to fire the clay into durable pottery.

Red Stone's large pots had since become well known in the neighboring town of Taos, a tourist center, where her work appeared in art galleries and at art markets. The yearly Santa Fe Indian Market drew collectors and dealers from across the United States and from other countries. Some of Red Stone's work was in the homes of international collectors. Aspen Deer respected her skill and was proud that his daughter had chosen to make pottery using the traditional methods of her people.

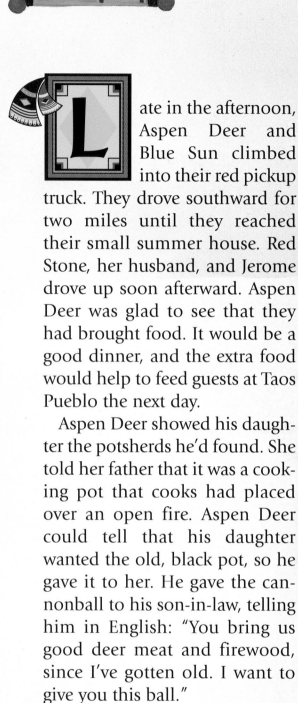L ate in the afternoon, Aspen Deer and Blue Sun climbed into their red pickup truck. They drove southward for two miles until they reached their small summer house. Red Stone, her husband, and Jerome drove up soon afterward. Aspen Deer was glad to see that they had brought food. It would be a good dinner, and the extra food would help to feed guests at Taos Pueblo the next day.

Aspen Deer showed his daughter the potsherds he'd found. She told her father that it was a cooking pot that cooks had placed over an open fire. Aspen Deer could tell that his daughter wanted the old, black pot, so he gave it to her. He gave the cannonball to his son-in-law, telling him in English: "You bring us good deer meat and firewood, since I've gotten old. I want to give you this ball."

he late summer sun cast long shadows over the green pastures where horses grazed. The family sat down and ate a meal of stew that Red Stone had made by grinding red peppers and mixing them with beef and pork. There would be plenty left to share at the celebration tomorrow. Jerome remarked that one of his favorite parts of festive events at the pueblo was the tasty stew.

After the meal, Aspen Deer sat in his favorite chair and dozed. Red Stone and Blue Sun sat on the porch to enjoy the warm evening. When Red Stone and her family left for the pueblo, Aspen Deer was still napping. The rumble of a truck engine soon woke him. He opened his eyes and recognized the truck. It belonged to his older son, Standing Buffalo. The young man had brought two friends with him from San Francisco, California. The trio would spend their vacation at Taos Pueblo. Aspen Deer's younger son, Moonlight on Aspens, arrived soon afterward. Blue Sun and Aspen Deer were happy to see their sons and pleased to welcome the visitors.

Standing Buffalo drummed and sang, with Aspen Deer and Moon-light joining in. Blue Sun taught Standing Buffalo's friend Lucy how to perform a Taos Pueblo social dance. Blue Sun told Lucy that these social dances were different from the ceremonial dances, which were sacred and secret from outsiders. But everyone could enjoy the social dances.

On San Antonio Day, women and men would dance the corn dance. Aspen Deer reflected on the *mielena*, the corn dance of the Pueblo people who lived in southern villages. Those dancers stood in two rows, one of men and one of women, each holding an ear of corn in his or her right hand. At Taos Pueblo, one man danced for every three to five female dancers.

Despite the name of the dance, no Taos dancer would carry corn on San Antonio Day. Instead women would hold fragrant evergreen boughs. Singers would sit around the big drum, which one man would beat while the other singers clapped in time. A man would shake a swishing rattle made from a gourd.

Aspen Deer remembered dancing as a young man. He had worn an eagle feather tied at the back of his long hair. At the beginning of a song, men had led the women in a circle. The women had dressed in colorful red, blue, and green dresses that left one shoulder bare. They had worn necklaces made from brown shells and pieces of turquoise.

It was nearly midnight when Aspen Deer and his sons stopped singing and drumming. Aspen Deer's arms were sore and tired from the shoveling followed by hours of drumming. But it had been a good day.

Tomorrow he would rest. Aspen Deer never went to watch the dances if he was not participating in them. But many of the teutho t'yono would be present to dance and to visit with relatives. Humo and Huokwimo would be vibrant with life.

Aspen Deer's morning prayer had guided him through the day. He had felt in harmony with people, the earth, the sky, and Mawholo. A round, white moon seemed to hang low above the eastern horizon. As the guests departed, Aspen Deer and Blue Sun looked out at the sky. The full white moon looked close enough to touch.

AFTERWORD

In the years since the arrival of the Europeans, Pueblo culture has faced many challenges. Yet the people have kept alive many of their traditions. Religious practices at Taos still center around the kiva. Many people still speak Tiwa in their daily lives. The ancient buildings, Humo and Huokwimo, continue to house people, and ritual dances celebrate events and mark the passage of the seasons.

But many changes have occurred as well. The Pueblo integrated elements of other cultures into their own. They quickly adopted ranching from settlers during Spanish rule. Christianity became part of Pueblo life. Christian feast days, such as San Antonio Day, became times to hold traditional Pueblo religious dances. Wheat, a crop brought by the Spaniards, enabled the cooking of wheat bread in hornos, another Spanish import. And these days, pickup trucks and cars help the Pueblo travel.

In the past 25 years, the population of Taos has grown. In the 1980s, the U.S. government began providing houses to Pueblo people living on the reservation surrounding Taos. Even so many people have left to find work. About half of the 3,000 registered members of the Taos Pueblo live off the reservation. Although many Pueblo Indians return for ceremonies and for special occasions, these far-off Pueblo people are unable to follow the traditional lifestyle every day. Kids raised away from the villages may not undergo kiva training. Young people grow up speaking both Tiwa and English or only English.

Life continues to change. High numbers of youngsters attend school. Some Native Americans doctor their own people and educate Pueblo schoolchildren in a culturally sensitive manner. Pueblo people have survived centuries of change. They continue to make sure that their lifeways endure.

Glossary

adobe: A type of clay soil found in Mexico and in dry parts of the United States. Sun-dried adobe bricks were used to build houses at Taos Pueblo.

animist: A person who believes that objects in nature and that acts of nature are filled with spiritual power.

archaeologist: A scientist who studies the material remains of past human life.

Blue Lake: A body of water located in the San Juan Mountains at an altitude over 11,500 feet. Sacred to the Taos Pueblo, the lake fits into Pueblo religious beliefs.

cacique: A religious leader and the head of the most important kiva at Taos Pueblo.

kiva: The Hopi Indian word for a ceremonial room that might be underground or above ground.

mission: A center where missionaries work to spread their beliefs.

missionary: A person sent out by a religious group to spread its beliefs to other people.

moiety: A half. Many Pueblo populations are divided into equal halves, with names such as Winter and Summer or Squash and Turquoise, for various functions, such as for ceremony and division of work.

pueblo: Meaning "town" in Spanish, this word was applied by Spanish settlers to the Native American villages of the Southwest. Native Americans of the Southwest are referred to as Pueblo Indians.

rawhide: Uncured animal hide that has been soaked and allowed to dry. The Pueblo traditionally use rawhide for rope and for drum covers.

Rio Grande: The river that flows through the states of New Mexico, Colorado, and Texas. Many pueblos are located along the river.

shrine: A sacred location where worshipers give prayers, cornmeal, and other offerings.

silica: A hard, glassy mineral found in clay. Silica is resistant to heat and electricity.

Southwest: The arid region in the southwestern corner of the United States, encompassing the states of New Mexico and Arizona. The deserts of northernmost Mexico are part of the same climate zone.

throwing stick: A foot-long oak stick resembling a club that is bulbous on one end.

thun: A white paint made from clay.

war chief: A leader in Taos Pueblo who, in former times, organized warfare. These days the war chief leads secular and ceremonial activities.

PRONUNCIATION GUIDE

adobe	ah-DOH-bee
cacique	kah-SEEK
Hernando de Alvarado	her-NAHN-doh day ahl-vah-RAH-doh
horno	OHR-noh
Humo	HOO-moh
Huokwimo	hoo-oh-kwee-moh
kiva	KEE-vah
Mawholo	MAH-hoh-loh
mesa	MAY-sah
moiety	MOY-eh-tee
pueblo	PWEH-bloh
Rio Grande	ree-oh GRAND
Sandia	sahn-DEE-ah
Santa Fe	sahn-tah FAY
silica	SIH-lih-cah
Taos	TOWSE
Tewa	TAY-wah
thun	THUHN
Tiwa	TEE-wah
Towa	TOE-wah
tuetho tíyono	TOO-thoh toy-OH-noh
viga	VEE-gah

FURTHER READING

Applegate, Frank. *Indians Stories from the Pueblo.* Bedford, MA: Applewood Books, 1994.

Brody, J. J. *A Day With a Mimbres.* Minneapolis: Runestone Press, 1999.

Cory, Steven. *Pueblo Indian.* Minneapolis: Lerner Publications Company, 1996.

Early, Theresa S. *New Mexico.* Minneapolis: Lerner Publications Company, 1993.

Echo-Hawk, Roger C. and **Walter R. Echo-Hawk.** *Battlefields and Burial Grounds.* Minneapolis: Lerner Publications Company, 1994.

Hayes, Joe, ed. *A Heart Full of Turquoise: Pueblo Indian Tales.* St. Paul: Mariposa Publishing Company, 1988.

Keegan, Marcia. *Pueblo Boy: Growing Up in Two Worlds.* New York: Cobblehill Books, 1991.

McDermott, Gerald. *Arrow to the Sun: A Pueblo Indian Tale.* New York: Viking Press, 1977.

Powell, Suzanne. *The Pueblos.* New York: Franklin Watts, 1993.

Swentzell, Rina. *Children of Clay. A Family of Pueblo Potters.* Minneapolis: Lerner Publications Company, 1992.

Young, Robert. *A Personal Tour of Mesa Verde.* Minneapolis: Lerner Publications Company, 1999.

Yue, Charlotte and **David Yue.** *The Pueblo.* New York: Houghton Mifflin, 1990.

Index

ABOUT THE
AUTHOR AND THE ILLUSTRATOR

Tito E. Naranjo, a Pueblo Indian, was born and raised in Santa Clara Pueblo, New Mexico. Mr. Naranjo has lived in and visited the Taos area for nearly 50 years. He attended Baylor University, New Mexico Highlands University, and the University of Utah. In 1992 Mr. Naranjo retired as a professor emeritus from New Mexico Highlands University. He continues to work as an artist, a writer, and a part-time teacher at the Taos branch of the University of New Mexico. Mr. Naranjo has authored three books and numerous articles. He lives in Mora, New Mexico, with his wife and son.

Giorgio Bacchin, a native of Milan, Italy, studied graphic arts in his hometown. After years of freelance graphic design, Mr. Bacchin has completely devoted himself to book illustration. His works have appeared in educational and trade publications.